BRIAN WHITTINGHAM, born and living in Glasgow, is a poet, playwright, fiction writer, editor and creative writing tutor. In 1994 he received the Yaddo residency, and in 2000 he won first prize in the Sunday Herald Short Story Competition. His poems and stories have been widely published in anthologies and magazines. A former steelworker/draughtsman, he performed his steel-working poems as part of the BBC's 'Ballad of the Big Ships Live' in Glasgow's Royal Concert Hall in 2007. He has performed and lectured in the UK, Europe and the USA, in places as diverse as beaches, universities, prisons, pubs, schools and colleges. He is currently a lecturer in creative writing at City of Glasgow College and was a visiting professor at Seattle University in 2011.

An ebook workshop to accompany this volume entitled *People Who Work Standing Up* is available on Kindle.

All photographs were taken by Brian Whittingham with the following exceptions:

The photograph accompanying 'School Trip' was taken by Jim Dunn (Glasgow Museums).

The photograph accompanying 'Histogram Man' was taken by Glen Campbell (Lightstalkers).

The photograph of Brian Whittingham and Sharon Cumberland accompanying the foreword was taken by Mara Adelman (Seattle University).

The photograph accompanying 'The Britannia Panopticon' was taken by Brian Whittingham with the permission of the Panopticon Theatre. The dresses belong to a private collection belonging to Judith Bowers and Graham Hunter.

Clocking In Clocking Out

Poems and Photographs
on the Subject of Work

BRIAN WHITTINGHAM

Luath Press Limited
EDINBURGH
www.luath.co.uk

First published 2012

ISBN: 978-1-908373-17-5

The publishers acknowledge the support of

ALBA | CHRUTHACHAIL

towards the publication of this volume.

The paper used in this book is recyclable. It is made
from low chlorine pulps produced in a low energy, low emissions
manner from renewable forests.

Printed and bound by
Bell & Bain Ltd., Glasgow

Typeset in 10.5 point Sabon by
3btype.com

For Cathie

Some of these poems have appeared in *The Old Man from Brooklyn and the Charing Cross Carpet*, published by Mariscat Press, *Septimus Pitt and the Grumbleoids*, published by Luath Press, *A Rose Loupt Oot* published by Smokestack Books, *Ergonomic Workstations and Spinning Teacans* and *Swiss Watches and the Ballroom Dancer* published by Taranus Books.

Contents

Foreword

Life grants nothing to us mortals without hard work.
Horace (65BC–8BC)

People who work sitting down get paid more than people who work standing up.
Ogden Nash (1902–1971)

ON SOME PEOPLE'S shelves Brian Whittingham's poetry sits next to Walt Whitman's poetry – an appropriate and telling juxtaposition since both are labour poets, writers whose sensibilities are attuned to the worker, the workplace, and the forces that circulate around the culture of labour in all its settings.

Whitman would have loved Whittingham's poems – the Glaswegian dialect, the straightforward description of setting and character, the human foibles exposed by a powerful balance between wit and sympathy. From his earliest forays into poetry – a chapbook called *Industrial Deafness*, a collection called *Ergonomic Workstations & Spinning Tea Cans* – Whittingham has been the bard of the shipyard, the chronicler of heavy labour in the ear-splitting, dangerous world of steel plate and rivets, ball-peen hammers and welding rods. Like Goldsmith's 'Sweet Auburn,' the Clydeside shipyards are gone now – as deserted as *The Deserted Village* – a fact that makes Whittingham's accounts, in works like his previous *Bunnets n Bowlers,* all the more valuable. Yet, like Whitman, Whittingham's poetry is not confined to the significance of his own workplaces, or to labourers of the past, but to the large phenomenon of labour as a window into the human character and condition.

Whittingham works in the very old tradition of labour poetry – a pedigree as ancient as poetry itself. Yet the category of 'labour poetry' may be unfamiliar outside of academia. We all know what to expect from 'love poetry,' for instance, or from 'religious poetry,' 'sentimental poetry' or 'occasional poetry.' But what, exactly, is 'labour poetry' and why does it deserve a category of its own?

One way to approach this question is to recognise that labour poetry is created in the space between survival and justice. Ever since Adam traded leisure for knowledge and got sent away from the Garden of Eden, mankind has had to 'purchase his bread by the sweat of his brow'. Horace sums up the human condition in the quotation above: no work, no survival. No matter how many virtues enrich the working life – usefulness, responsibility, challenge, self-respect – the fact remains that work keeps the wolf from the door. To work is, first and foremost, to survive.

Ogden Nash captures another dimension of the human condition when, in the second quotation above, he conjures up the political reality that some jobs are easier and better compensated than others. Nash implies that the cultural capital of having the right gender, education, race or parentage creates social class distinctions characterized by exploitation – 'the rich get richer and the poor get poorer' to quote an old Depression era song. In Nash's observation, sitting down is an image that represents all the advantages of white collar work: higher pay, social mobility, prestige, larger homes, better education for children, better food. Likewise, standing up is an image that represents all the disadvantages of blue collar work: lower pay, loss of autonomy, vulnerability to exploitation, lack of voice in decisions that affect quality of life – not to mention fewer years of education, smaller homes, scarcer food, and hurting feet (and hands, and spines, and ears, and lungs...). We all know that work is more nuanced than the white/blue divide: white collar workers are subject to high levels of stress; blue collar workers often achieve job security and satisfaction. Yet justice, or the lack of it, is a major subtext of labour poetry.

Brian Whittingham's poetry falls squarely in the category of poetry that examines labour from the two angles of survival and justice, and in this his ancestors are Homer and the ancient oral poets, who used dactylic hexameters to describe the Trojan War and the human toll and toil of conflict both for men on the battlefield and for women suffering the deprivations of war. Whittingham is also in the tradition of labour poets like Hesiod, Theocritus, and Virgil. Hesiod, in 650BC wrote the 800 lines of verse in *Works and Days* to persuade his wastrel brother to engage in the virtues of farming. Theocritus' *Idylls,* written in the third century BC, are all about shepherds, cattle herders, housewives and veterans suffering the injustice of denied benefits for military service. Theocritus is credited with the invention of pastoral poetry, which is associated with Arcadia, idealised landscapes, and rosy-cheeked lads and lasses playing pan pipes under low-hanging boughs – but pastoral poetry has its origins in real shepherds and real work. One of the most famous labour poems from ancient times is Virgil's *Georgics,* which explains planting and harvesting with such accuracy that if a meteor hit the earth and threatened mankind with extinction, the human race could re-start itself with a single copy of Virgil's poem of instruction for the would-be farmer.

Whittingham can also claim Shakespeare as a precursor, since the Bard invariably includes a group of servants, fools and labourers to provide the low humour that mirrors the high matters of the noble and powerful protagonists. Often the real truth, plainly stated or sung in ditties, is given to Shakespeare's humble labourers who either see through the pretensions of kings or give comic relief by imitating their 'betters'. Shakespeare's audience, like Whittingham's readers, recognise both the wisdom of ordinary folk as well as the foolish or dangerous ambitions of their bosses.

In more recent centuries, Goldsmith and William Blake used poetry to warn of the effects of the industrial revolution – the 'dark satanic mills' – and unjust laws such as the Enclosures, which show the reader how 'the rich man's joys increase, the poor's decay' when farms, villages and livelihoods are destroyed to make way for private gardens. Whittingham's poems imply the critique that these poets made explicit, telling, in his unadorned way, the stories of secretaries, clowns, athletes and hangmen whose life situations are shaped by the large forces of society lurking in the background, imposing the necessities and difficulties that bring tension to the poems as well as the observed lives. Whittingham takes his material from the found world, reconstructing those realities through language and imagination – but his stories are as grounded in actuality as those of Theocritus, Hesiod and Shakespeare.

Whittingham is also working in the tradition of Wordsworth and Coleridge, who reclaimed poetry from the lofty heights of formalism with *Lyrical Ballads* and returned to the concerns of ordinary men and women going about the business of living. Wordsworth's Preface to *Lyrical Ballads* is the manifesto that initiated the Romantic Movement by extolling the language of the ordinary person, ie the one who works rather than the one who lives on inherited wealth. Precursor to the Romantic Movement – and supreme among the labour poets – is Robert Burns, whose vivid dialect and accounts of the Scottish people and landscape established the model for all writers who care about capturing the essence of a culture through the voice of the folk who live in it, while probing the depths and shallows of human character. Whittingham is truly Burns' descendant in his use of dialect and his acute eye for the humour and oddities that surround him, not only in Glasgow, but in his travels. Just as Burns wrote through the lens of anticlerical republicanism, Whittingham has a gimlet eye for the privileged – those who gain their power through inheritance or tradition. It is small wonder that Whittingham is inspired by his travels to America, and the free-wheeling open culture that bows to movie stars and athletes rather than to kings and bishops.

To come closer to the original question, labour poetry is the poetry of work, whether it addresses what people do to survive or whether it addresses the injustices or tensions that arise from inequalities in the workplace. The poets who write about labour and labourers – what they do, how they do it, where and when they work, and the culture they create as they work – form a distinctive group. Philip Levine, Muriel Rukeyser, Gwendolyn Brooks, Rita Dove and the Carol Ann Duffy of *The World's Wives* – to name only a few contemporary poets – continue to develop the range and reach of labour poetry. Brian Whittingham, in this collection, adds to his own range and reach, and increases the reader's insight into those who work standing up. The writing of poetry is, itself, hard work – work that calls for steady practice, constant polishing and mastery of skills that make the worker's hand invisible. The Greek word for 'poet' is translated as 'maker' – one who makes something, a craftsman. A poem is a made thing, like a shoe or a ship, which is why poets talk about the 'craft' of poetry writing. Brian Whittingham has gone from working in a shipyard to drafting, to driving a taxi, to writing poetry – a transition that seems natural to those who understand that poetry is labour. Why does labour poetry deserve a category of its own? Because labour poets like Brian Whittingham – working in a tradition that stretches back to Homer – show us something important about ourselves by writing about what we do to keep the wolf from the door.

Dr Sharon Cumberland
Director, Creative Writing Program.
Seattle University.

Brian Whittingham and Sharon Cumberland at Park Place Books, Kirkland, Seattle

Introduction

PUSHEM & SLOGGEM, Bluffum & Doemdown, Dodger & Scampit, Snatchem & Graball, Smeeriton & Leavit, Makehaste & Sloggit, and Rushton & Co. were the painting and decorating companies I was introduced to with my first taste of reading labour writing, in the novel *The Ragged Trousered Philanthropists* by Robert Tressell. Being a young apprentice I was enthralled by the authenticity captured by the writer, of bosses and workers, poverty and wealth, employment and unemployment, socialism and capitalism, etc. that resulted in a lifelong interest in labour writing.

When someone asks, 'What do you do?' we tend to define ourselves by the job of work that we do, or don't do, – as society generally does. As if our work situation is the sum total of who we are.

Over the years I have written about my own working experiences as a steelworker, a fabrication inspector, a draughtsman, a drawing office manager, a taxi driver and various other in-between jobs, because I've always been fascinated by the broader brush strokes of labour and all its implications. I have been intrigued by the plethora of interesting ways by which people earn their living and I have read and enjoyed many works of writers setting their writings in a labour setting, amongst which are *Dear Green Place* by Archie Hind, *Devil's Carousel* by Jeff Torrington, *Germinal* by Emile Zola, *Goodstone* by Fred Voss, *What Work Is* by Philip Levine and *Bus Conductor Hines* by James Kelman.

My increasing curiosity over the years led me to the United States as a visiting professor at Seattle University during which time I explored what Americans refer to as 'Labour Poetry' and my subsequent experience of reading and getting into the mindset of labour poetry has resulted in my pulling together *Clocking In Clocking Out.*

This is a collection where every poem has a connection with people doing a job of work, directly or indirectly, or people having leisure time away from a job of work, and even then, there is usually someone working to service them. The poems are only dipping into the subject by recording my own observations of these happenings in action. They are not autobiographical but are part of my own personal biography of what I've seen and experienced of others and labour.

I've included photographs that I've taken along the way, to reflect on what the poems are saying. I recently returned to B&W photography and with my interest in picture-taking rekindled, decided on pictures that both complimented their B&W format along with having something extra to say about the poems they partner. I write in images, so to me, these photographs seem a natural extension to my writing voice.

The collection includes a diverse range of work related experiences including jobs such as boxers, hangmen, hairdressers, performance artists, poets, steelworkers, dancers, train drivers, models, teachers, chaplains, the unemployed and so on.

A few years ago I read *Catch: A Fishmonger's Guide to Greatness*, a book that was written by the fishmongers at Seattle's Pike Place Fish Market. I also interviewed a few of the fishmongers who firmly believed in worker empowerment and working on how better to serve customers, co-workers and ultimately yourself. Doing what may be seen by some as a mundane job, these fishmongers have written motivational books and have videos that have been used in life coaching and as training resources.

This intrigued me and along with encouragement from Sharon Cumberland, an American poet and the present Director of the Creative Writing Program at Seattle University, whom I became friends with when I got my first writing fellowship at YADDO, an artist's retreat in upstate New York in 1994, I've explored the world of labour writing.

Being a poet, having a solitary disposition and having served an engineering apprenticeship meant I naturally have watched people doing jobs with a curious eye. Being a tradesman (shop floor and office worker) means I've noticed the territory of doing both and have recorded what I've experienced.

Along the journey of our working lives, our heads become filled with the useless minute detail of the labour we've been touched by. Useless now, but at the time, without even thinking, we've been experts at the minutiae of past labours. I recently gave a woman at the Titan Crane visitor's centre a handful of books and she, without thinking, started boxing them together as if shuffling a pack of cards, then remarked she'd once worked in a printers and an old habit was kicking in after so many years had elapsed. How many of us do such things?

Have you ever noticed the joiner who makes sure all screw head slots are of the same orientation when fixing panelling to walls, or the barmaid balancing pint tumblers on top of each other whilst pouring drinks from three taps simultaneously, or the post office clerk who knows the answers to the multitude of questions the public throw at them and always answer with a smile. All actions carried out with barely a thought about the process because that's what they do. Of course, there are also the workers who couldn't care a jot about the quality of the work they produce and only too readily show this in their attitude towards their work and to others who are misfortunate enough to encounter them during their working day. As the old saying goes, it takes all kinds.

I've worked in a variety of jobs, have been unemployed a number of times, sometimes getting redundancy payment, sometimes not, and now work as a Further Education College lecturer, professor and writer.

I've worked all sorts of hours, bare time, overtime, time and a half, double time, dayshift, nightshift, unsociable hours, more hours than the rats. I've worked in union closed shops, non-union shops, been involved in trade-union work-ins, and been on countless Right to Work demonstrations in my younger years.

Labour leaves not one of us untouched during our life. A mother goes into labour when a child is born, and so it goes on till our dying day. At school we prepare for doing a job of labour. During our apprenticeship or University or College years, we prepare in more detail for it. Or if we've been unfortunate enough never to have worked and had a healthy income then we've been dealt a cruel hand indeed because we suffer the repercussions in spadefuls. Sometimes, somewhere along the line we think we don't use the fruits of our studies, our learning, as we veer off in new directions. 'What good did such and such do me?' we ask when our new job doesn't require a particular skill we've painstakingly learned. However, we have learned and in doing so have enriched ourselves as human beings. Or have we?

Whatever our preparation or lack of it entails, we, in the main, end up doing a variety of jobs. In the course of our working lives we earn thousands upon thousands of pounds yet when we are old we can invariably end up financially still in the doldrums. Strange isn't it?

Then, when we reach a certain age we retire and try to live without our work. Some of us do so with great pleasure as the physical and mental burden of the job is lifted from us and maybe, just maybe, we have financial security. Others just wilt and die because they seem to have little purpose and no further goals to achieve or are just plain worried about the perception of an insecure future.

I once asked a guy I worked beside, 'Do you think a company misses a worker when they leave?' He diverted my gaze towards a plaque on the wall of his office. It displayed a poem telling the story of how much a worker is missed by using the analogy of putting your hand into a bucket of water, then taking it out and looking to see what difference it made. Not a jot.

Most of the poems I've written are about men in work because, being a West of Scotland male, I've worked in predominantly male environments, through no conscious choosing of my own. I have recorded some female work experiences, I doubt anyone worked harder than my mother's generation, and I know if someone else were to write their version of a labour collection the mix would be different again. Why don't you try? My challenge to you is to write five labour poems from your own experiences of working life. Just for the sheer pleasure of doing so. Who knows? You may surprise yourself when you share your work with others.

Whatever you get from this collection, I hope it makes you consider the world of labour through fresh eyes and a better appreciation for something that takes up so much of our lives.

The Britannia Panopticon

Centre-stage, a woman, beside a GOD SAVE THE KING
  poster,
all petticoats and lace,
tells of the Music Hall's history –

– the audience of shipyard workers
who threw nuts and bolts at disappointing acts.
The boys who urinated from the balcony
on the orchestra below
and THE GREAT RUBINI –
who beheaded a lady every evening at 8 pm ... and so on.

The MC with his fake upturned moustache
and stick on side-whiskers
assures us we're in for
a splendiferous cornucopia of afternoon delights
as he introduces each act
with alliterative attacks of alarming alacrity.

ORDER – ORDER!

Banging his gavel
he culminates each announcement
heralding a teaming torrent of tempting talent
for our delight and delectation!

The Great Aziz with the tux and a toothpaste smile,
who, like an exotic geisha,
fans his pack of cards that appear from nowhere.

The piper who skirls his Scottish melodies
marching on the spot
while winking at the girls in the front row

The Shirley Temple diva
who laments
that her daddy wouldn't buy her a bow-wow!

And the Harry Lauder lookalike
who pays homage to Sinatra
by singing 'Fly me to Dunoon.'

Onstage, the full company take their final bows
in front of the assorted audience
who have wandered in off the street.

We stomp, cheer, whistle and clap ...
stowed to the gunnels with rumbustiousness.

At the UCS Work-in

The workers were supported
with impromptu dinner time shows
in the canteen where they sat at long benches
eating soup from bowls
like extras in an Oliver Twist movie.

One day, a man dressed in a leopard-skin leotard
stood on top of such a table,
squatted slightly, with hands
gripping his knees
as a comrade clamped
what looked like
a giant piece of elastic between Leotard Man's teeth.

The comrade proceeded
to walk the length of the canteen
and as the elastic stretched
he informed us all
that what leotard man had in his mouth
was heavy duty industrial knicker elastic,
that when released,
would travel at a velocity of 90 mph
and smash into Leotard Man's face
with a force of 100 lbs per square inch.

When the comrade stopped at the top end of the canteen,
the knicker elastic, taut above the diner's heads,
with Leotard Man grimacing,
the elastic clenched in tightly shut jaws

his comrade asked *'Are – you – ready?'*

Leotard man replied *'Yes!'*

at which the elastic
whipped across the heads of diving diners
all wearing smiles of survival.

The next day –
on the same table,
there was a basket
of red roses from John & Yoko –
an altogether more peaceful affair.

Dusting Lilies

For five Euro we get to see Monet's house
policed by green jacketed attendants
wearing water-lily ties and stern faces,
keeping lookout
as behind their backs, multi-coloured climbing roses
seem to be ever so slowly
gobbling up the very house itself.

We stroll at a pace that seems appropriate
past the flowerbeds
with sunflowers and carnations and marigolds,
and nasturtiums and cacti and delphiniums and so forth

to arrive at the pond
traversed with Japanese footbridges
crammed with camera toting tourists
taking innumerable snaps of the lilies
that Monet's gardener would dust soot from,
that came from passing trains,
so the master could capture them in pristine condition.

The picture takers
have little regard for their fellow photographers
as they step into each others memories.
so eager to record, their being in the presence of genius.

In Glasgow the Poet was a Snowflake

who wore a white boilersuit
covered in cotton wool balls.

His job was to climb to the top
of the architect's
large-scale steel structured Christmas-tree.

Once there, other snowflakes
would climb to various positions in the tree
swinging large cotton wool balls
to and fro.

Street theatre it was called.

Snowflakes on the ground
were to hand out sheets of paper
to a puzzled public
who were asked to write lines of poetry.

The snowflakes on the ground
would then pass the pieces of paper
to the other snowflakes
making their way to the poet at the top

who would compose a poem
then shape his paper
into an origami paper plane
becoming a symbolic snowflake
he would then throw to the crowd.

The idea being the public would unfold the poem
and the connection would be made
so to speak.

And, as this council carnival of culture
tried vainly to hit the spot
a young family
was seen to walk away
shaking their heads
with the father saying to the mother ...

'An know whit the best of it all is?
they'll get fuckin' paid fur that so they wull.'

Dressing Down

Friday was designated dressing-down-day.

In the offices, the staff,
for some this meant loosening their ties.
For others, this meant wearing no tie.
For others, this meant wearing denims.

For others, this meant
they could dress as if
they were at Bondi beach
for their summer vacation.

The shop-floor,
if they were to have such a thing,
would probably have had a
a dressing-up-day
as they always wore suits and ties
when they visited Human Resources.

If you wore a tie on a Friday
it was considered inappropriate.
If you didn't wear a tie mid-week
it was considered inappropriate.

The new-broom of an M.D.
banned dressing-down-day
to the history books
and everyone was happy once again.

The carrot of self-expression
that had been dangled in front of them,
they'd been reluctant to consume.

The 7th Inning Stretch and all

Vendors thread stairways, yellow shirted ants
with trays of lemonade balanced on heads,
crates of beer slung round necks,
baskets of soda hung over shoulders.

They theatrically throw bags of peanuts
over under arm.
Patrons pass dollar bills along their row.

And the crowd, always eating, drinking
or taking part in overhead video games.

till the 7th inning's stretch
where children and adults follow the bouncing ball
singing 'Take me out to the ballgame,'

Then the fan's lethargy
disturbed by expectation as *Ichiro Suzuki*
limbers up bending and stretching
and swinging his bat across the back of his shoulders
before taking position at Home Plate.

The stadium's organ music pumps up the volume.
Didididledee – didididledee – didididledee!

As *Ichiro* prepares, standing on tiptoes
like a matador ready for the kill,
with his right arm extended,
bat held vertical, he stands taking his own time

Kids in the crowd prepare their mitts
in anticipation of catching their dreams.

The relief pitchers watch from the Bullpen,
they chew sunflower seeds
spit spit spitting empty shells –
waiting for *their* chance.

Ichiro relaxes into his swing

The pitcher crouches slightly with leg crossed
as if a stork frozen in the moment.

Unleashes his 94 mph fastball
that cracks off *Ichiro's* swinging bat,
hitting a home run
as every kid's dream is realised,
the ball soaring through the night air like a missile
and all the Red-Sox can do is helplessly watch
while the Mariners jog leisurely round the bases
and smiling the smiles of magicians
who know, for that moment,
they have hit the spot yet again.

Good Night Driver

The late night-driver
fills in his time-sheet
to a chorus of

'Whit's the haud up big man?
We've got our fuckin' beds to go tae.'

and one guy pounds the Perspex screen
howling for the driver to get his arse into gear
and three couples
stomp on paying four fares
and a man with eyelids
like a Thunderbird's puppet
states to no one in particular
that THEY never pay their fare – By the way!
as a bevvied lady
in a short green skirt
with matching jacket
argues with the partner of the 'By the way' man
and the Perspex pounder
screams at the non-payers
'Come oan tae fuck! We've goat our beds to go tae!'

and the late night bus smoulders

like a volcano waiting to erupt!

Robert the Bruce

He's a dealer in the past
for customers in the present.

Military medals, hats, regimental badges, coins.

His patch is a stall at the Barras
and his business card tells me he's Robert the Bruce.

So – I have the phone number of Robert the Bruce.

He tells me,
'They banned the wearing of the kilt,
apart from the military that is,
The Black Watch and such.
A lot of the regiments
have connections with the islands,
Benbecula, for example, still has an army base.'

'What's it like there?'

'It's that windy, there are no trees. None of these islands have
trees.'

'Sounds desolate.'

'Not desolate, beautiful, do you know
the beaches are as white as ...'

he ponders trying to find the appropriate analogy
then looking to the wedding stall across the way

'as white as that bride's dress hanging there,'
he points to make sure I get it

and a small old bent man beside me
wearing a Glengarry, tweed jacket, kilt,
sporran, white hose with sgian dubh
and black brogues, tugs my sleeve.

'There's a tree in Barra,' he informs me
as if he's just let slip a government secret.

The George Square Tea Dance

On frosty tar-macadam ground,
dancers swing
amongst a spattering of fluttering pigeons.

Icy breaths lick air.

Ladies, gents, teens and children
dressed in shoes, boots, trainers
coats, heavy jackets
woolly hats, bunnets, baseball caps
and scarves

and one lady wears a mock leopard skin fur,
carries a shopping bag
as she jerks and jitterbugs
with a grey haired gent in denims and anorak
that she periodically gives a high-five to
each time
the band's rhythm section socks it to them.

And another man has a little girl
standing on top of his feet.

He clasps her hand with his,
supports her back with his other hand's flattened palm
and they birl and wheech about
like there's no tomorrow.

Steaming tea and fruit scones
and smiles dancing on everyone's' faces.

With two professionals
weaving in and out of the crowd showing
how it should be done,
the lady with the billowing polka dot dress
and the pink carnation in her buttonhole
and the man with the dinner suit and black patent shoes
Both wearing their widest fixed ballroom smiles.

In the West of Scotland

The Fab-Four tribute band
murder *All You Need is Love*
in the bowling club
lubricated by cheap firewater
and mirror-ball lighting.

Silver tinted ladies
at the committee table
link arms
smile, sway from side to side.

Separated by tables
stowed with empty tumblers.
An evening for serious swallying.

Their bookend partners
sit opposite, stone faced,
fingers wrapped around pint glasses

their only movement
being the lifting and lowering of their drinks.

Momentarily though,
one seems to forget his place
in the great scheme of things

and ever so slightly
can be seen, tapping the ball of his foot
to the beat of the music.

Old Subway Dreams

My father settles down in his chair,
studies form with his magnifying glass
scanning the racing section of the Evening Times.

On my weekly visit to his world,
I again, search for his conversation.

'Do you miss your work?'

'I don't miss it, I dream it.'
he replies, studying form.

He tells me fragments.

Tunnel Black

A Copeland Rd driver
ignoring safety regulations
crushed to death when he toppled out the door.

Needled Light

A phantom balloon floating by
like a dismembered head.

Eye straining

A woman who fell
in front of his stationary train.
A daily rag making him a hero.
'Never got a penny for that story!'
he tells me yet again.
A faded newspaper cutting.

Failed Signals

Lord Wintergreen who smelled rather strange.
The Skipper who held green lights all the way.
Drivers caught short, who would piss into black.

A Cessnock ghost.

Workmen, who bonded themselves
to the tunnel's curves as the trains hurtled past
rattling and clattering before being swallowed by darkness.

It was then I remembered how
he used to sit for hours
shining the buttons on his jacket
with Brasso and a shield slid behind the buttons
making sure there wasn't a blemish
on the olive green of the pristine uniform.

The Weight of Words

The retired professor is a sidewalk-philosopher
and once a week he drives
to his Letter-Press class, where each student
goes back in time, creating individual works of art.

In class, a colleague makes an artist's book,
her thoughts, on concertina pages, connected with gold thread
    stitches.

For *his* project, the professor has written a poem,
to be printed on once discarded envelopes.
With tweezers, he selects *10-point Bembo type,* from the *type
    case,*
as if a surgeon performing a delicate operation.

He deftly places each letter,
each punctuation mark, each shim and each spacer,
and ties his composition taut with string.

He rests his composed poem on a *galley,*
a metal tray that he lifts like a baker lifting a too heavy cake.

He sets it on the CHANDLER & PRICE.
Its flywheel spins slowly first
then faster and faster with its leather drive belt whirring
as the press, clatters and rattles
and the professor feeds his paper
like a man possessed, each hand doing its separate job
in time with the machine's mechanical rhythm
that lets the inked type make its impression.

Cachunk – Cachunk – Cachunk – Cachunk – Cachunk.

Once finished, he takes apart the composed poem,
the letters and punctuation disappearing again
into the body of the open type case.

And all he is left with is each envelope having
the weight of his final choice of words
and the satisfaction of finding another piece of himself in the
    process.

The Boxer

To the beeps of the electronic till
ringing sales
faster than the Sonny Liston knockout.

The Greatest, sits beside his assistant
who sticks pre-autographed labels
into books piled high on the signing table.

The books with snaps that show
a young man floating and stinging.

Admirers crouch beside
the boxer with smiling eyes
as they get their photos taken
with this famous personality
while he mechanically shakes their hands.

Then Ali slowly rises
amid the barrage of camera flashes
jabbing the bookstore's interior.

His dark body and white shirt
mimic a boxer's crouch
with his fists half-clenched
and a customer adopts the same pose
respectfully playing the game
mock bobbing and weaving on the spot.

The Greatest sits sluggishly down
and when given a book to sign in his own hand
he clumsily clutches a pen
and his scrawled signature
is written as if in slow motion.

The bookstore assistants watch
like seconds in the corner
too late to throw in the towel.

The Evangelist

The Argyle St evangelist
informs the teeming throng
of festive Saturday shoppers
that he was speaking to God
that morning.

He cradles his microphone
as if he had a direct line,
shrouding each word carefully

His colleague frantically waves
a placard above his head
as if passing shoppers
are about to miss the second coming.

And as he does so
the placard waver advises
the people with busy city centre faces
dragging
children's Christmas dreams by the hand
whilst jostling for pole position
like a panic stricken crowd in a disaster movie

SHOUTING

'We are all sinners, brothers and sisters,
all sinners,
but remember – we have to bind
we have to rebuke Satan's temptations
we have to look to the guidance of God.'

Rosie the Riveter

The old lady sits proud
at the Washington Woman's trade-fair.

Behind a table laden with bits of her past,
photographs of a young Rosie
wearing her bib overalls
and spotted handkerchief knotted on her head
and her, *We Can Do It*, smile
and flexing her arm muscle
with her rolled up sleeve, strongwoman style.

She and her friends tell tales of being
riveters, welders, sheet-metal workers,
with money in their pockets and steel in their souls.
One tells of her male foreman
who welcomed her with
'I aint never worked with no fucking woman,'
then sniggered at her pristine tool belt,
that she backed her car over to make it look used
so the ridicule would abate.

* * *

Across the passageway
lady carpenters stand behind benches
to demonstrate how to make stools.
The carpenters show how wood
gets cut and planed and smoothed and glued and nailed,
to the young women who've never experienced
how tactile the tangible putting together of things can be.

The students in line are excited

and hand their pre-cut wood pieces
to the carpenters eager to pass on their skills
to the young novices,
some of whom delicately tap tap tap
the nails with their hammers held awkwardly,
tap tap tap
tap tap tap

Then, the finished stool,
the young women are ready to decorate.
They stick multi coloured plastic flowers
and shapes and letters,
one proudly spells out her name
and wears a smile of deep satisfaction.

Hanging Frank

A man called Frank tells death watch tales
to the listening camera

tells of his sadness to see the end of an era at hand.

Reminiscing, he demonstrates
a length of rope shaping it into a noose

10' 6" long, white Italian hemp, ¾" diameter
lined with soft calf leather around the neck area.

He shows how the executioner would place it
over the hood on the condemned
preventing trapdoor back draught blowing the hood off
preventing the prisoner seeing final seconds.

    Frank remembers the time
    a young prisoner's tear trickled below the hood.

    Frank remembers the time
    a prisoner ran, his arms strapped, halted by a rugby tackle.

    Frank remembers birthday cards
    passed into the condemned cell celebrating a 21st.

He describes how the hangman would calculate the weight
height distance of drop ratio and adjust his rope accordingly.

A large brown pot of tea
and chats about any subject apart from the obvious.

Frank describes the execution chamber

The hanging beam designed to take up to three prisoners at a
    time.

The trapdoor with safety planks
to support the guards who steadied the prisoner prior to his fall.

The snapping of the 2nd and 3rd vertebrae.

Instantaneous.

The body buried within prison grounds, property of the state.

And Frank assures listeners there was no truth
in the rumour that a fellow executioner,
Albert Pierpoint, had an obsession with knots.

'A nicer man you couldn't wish to meet.'
Frank tells us with the sincerest of smiles.

Grez Cemetry

Lizards scuttle under warm marble slabs.

An attendant shades his eyes from the midday sun,
discreetly keeps order
in amongst rows of pristine tombs.

beside the gold letter legend

eternalle regrette a notre ami

Weeping angels.
Praying Madonnas.
Vases of red roses and white lilies.
Dove figurines.
A motor cyclist jumping.
Open paged marble books
and an extinguished lamp.

A musical stave with soaring notes.

To a backdrop of a life size sculpture
of Christ's crucifixion
with rust streaks from his nails
looking like brown blood,
his torso, flaking white paint
and a serpent snaking the base of the cross.

Yellow and black striped bumble bees
swarm nodding lavender
that fills the air with its pungent scent.

The Retired Puppeteer

The retired puppeteer
who looks like Mister Punch
tells us, his audience

'At night, the ancient puppeteers
stored the puppets' heads
separate from their bodies ...
made from wood you see – a living thing.'

He tells us

'In the beginning before the puppets,
even before writing,
storytellers in Egypt, Greece, India and China
told their tales
with movement of the hands.'
He demonstrates.

He slowly spreads extended fingers
to represent a rising sun.
His hands scribe a circle in the air
to represent the earth.
He waggles dragging fingers
to represent a free-flowing river.

He prompts us to follow suit
with his next example
and, as if manipulated by strings from above,
we all place palm on palm
under our inclined heads
and mimic sleeping a slumbering sleep.
All the while his retired slack stringed marionettes

slouch in the lecture theatre's corner
watching us with hooded eyes
like half drunk actors frozen offstage
awaiting their cue to come to life.

The History of Alex Morrison

Born in 1916.

'There were twelve of us
but I'm the only one left.
Ninety three I am ... did you know that son?'

Neatly labelled folders
overflow with yesterdays surrounding Alex. Fading newspapers,
articles, photographs, clippings and crystal memories.

'There would be people in Old Snodgrass's field
who stood too near the river's edge.
They got soaked with the wash from the launch,
not me though,
I knew to stand well back.' He winks as he says this.

'It was a penny for a bag of chocolates in those days ... did you
      know that son?'

The interviewer asks about the QE2
but Alex carries on his independent narrative,
'The Empress of Britain – 1931. Sheee was a beautiful ship –
you know, one day the Captain waved at me from the bridge,
what a sight, if he'd shook my hand I wouldn't have washed it.'

Alex opens a homemade wooden box.
'This came from a piece of the QE2's slipways when she was
      launched.'
He looks at it in wonder,
'Made this myself ... did you know that son?'

Memories spill from everything he touches.

'They were great times then, no one had a motor car,
my brother was a carpenter, the yards were full of families,
fathers and sons and uncles
and, women doing the French Polishing,
and Snodgrass was the place to see ships ... did you know that
    son?'

'The Carmania, The Lusitania, The Aquitania, The Britannia
and the QE2 *– I mind someone sneaked me into Browns*
the time they laid the keel.'

'I touched it with my hand.'
He smiles like a mischievous schoolboy.

The cameraman smiles back.
His camera records.

Looking for Business

At midnight on Christmas Eve
in mid stride
she automatically repaints her red lipstick lips
as she runs across the road.

Clacking killer heels on black.

An unseen driver rolls down his window,
his engine purrs to a halt
in the street shaded
with night frost and ever so thin ice.

And with her short suede skirt
and shiny black bag
she tips her bleached blond head down
towards the stranger in the car.

The Illusionist

The Coney Island illusionist
stood in his showman's pulpit
on the sidewalk
outside his tented pavilion.

The man from New York
hollered about the mysteries
that would be revealed
for an entrance fee of only $1

He explained the wonders of
NO MIDDLE MYRTLE
THE PENGUIN GIRL
and THE WOMAN WITH FOUR LEGS

Unable to resist, we were taken
inside where he tried his best
to make the faded life-
size photographs appear interesting

by telling us
THE HUMAN VOLCANO
and THE TATOOED BEARDED LADY
led fulfilled lives

And sensing out disappointment
at not seeing these human freaks
in the flesh
he leapt on a nearby stage

turning a cane into a silk kerchief
cutting a rope in two
then joining it back together again

and we stood fast
forgetting how to applaud

as he informed no one in particular

'I'd better slow down
the G forces are killing them!'

Bares and Broncs

At the Ellensburg rodeo.

It's raining for the first time in years.
The wetness shines on the marshal's oilskins.
Water drips from the rims of their Stetsons
as their horses trot round the muddy arena.

In the bucking chute,
Cowboys, delicately saddle up *Tumbling Lady*.
The filly doesn't take too kindly to being harnessed.
She bucks, whinnies, stomps.

Waiting for his ride
is Chuck Cardoza, a local wrangler.
He prepares his neck brace
and wraps his padded body protector tighter
as he mimes his riding technique
tugging imaginary reins tight
and jerking, getting ready to go with the flow.

He slowly climbs up on the chute
and gingerly sits astride *Tumbling Lady's* saddle
clenching the braided reins with one hand
and slipping his boots into the swinging stirrups.

His free arm outstretched, hand held high.

The gate is thrown open, cowboys leap clear,
Tumbling Lady explodes from the chute.

The horse erupts into a bucking frenzy
as Chuck attempts to find its rhythm.
he clings on grimly, his hat spinning from his head.

With short, sharp kicks
the filly bounds and springs and finally shakes off Chuck,
whose back arches like that of a discarded rag doll.

A dazed Chuck Cardoza regains his feet
and staggers, like a drunken John Wayne,
back towards the crowd
who half heartedly applaud his valiant attempt.

Chuck clenches his fist and punches the air in anger.

Tumbling Lady canters back to the stables,
munches on a bale of hay, unconcerned,
with the cowboy who has failed to earn his spurs.

The Indians from Tillicum Village

... welcome the 35$ a trip tourists of today.
Their launch clunking the pier
on Blake Island State Park.

The tourists with assorted cameras
walk along the path
strewn with discarded clam shells
crunching under their feet,
to be greeted by Indian Braves
serving cartons of clams from steaming pots.

The tourists sip the broth
swallow their clams
and throw away shells onto the path
observing island tradition.

The path winds through totem poles
each topped with a raven's head.

The tourists enter the longhouse
styled in the fashion
of an ancient communal dwelling.

The tourists shuffle along their line
helping themselves
to red potatoes and mixed salad.

An Indian serves a small portion
of Alaskan salmon baked
on cedar stakes around an alder fire.

Once seated at tables around a stage
the *Dance on the Wind* begins.

The Indians prance around the stage
in costumes of beads, feathers and furs.

They do the *Ancestral Dance*
choreographed to perfection
as if to resurrect legends
of times long gone.

Once entertained the tourists
loop into the craft shop
for Native American knickknacks.

They pose for photos with the Indian
who wears an eagle-head mask
and pulls strings clacking its beak.

The launch clunks the pier on the Indian Island
with a fresh batch of tourists
who make ready
for the walk along the clam shell path.

The Irish Alaskan

In the Seattle hotel lobby
he sticks his head outside the window,
has another draw on his cigarette.

He tells me about his president ...

'A village idiot.
If you want a war
put a Texan in the White House.
Johnston with Vietnam
Bush 1 with Desert Storm
Bush 2 with Iraq.
Looking after their oil-buddies
that's all their doing.'

He tells me about his home ...

'In Anchorage, the weather is so bad
it's like clouds are walking the streets.
Very depressing.'

He tells me about his work ...

'I'm a bum.
I don't work.
That's what my father calls someone who doesn't work,
a bum ... so ... I'm a bum.

He tells me about the cops ...

'Village idiots also,
like little children carrying guns,
they threw me in jail because I had some money,
reckoned I was a member of Al Qaeda,
I mean,
do I look like an Arab?'

He tells me about the constitution ...

'They say it's outdated.
What's outdated about it man?
The law's the law.
Right from wrong don't get outdated,
do it?'

He sticks his head outside the window,
has another draw on his cigarette.

The Hospital Chaplain

Ex-Squadron Leader Bradshaw
descends into the ward.
Introduces himself to patients
with his firm RAF handshake.

The wee man puffs his barrel chest.
Smiles his reverential smile.
Mixes his potion
of instant ministerial sincerity.

He pulls up his trouser leg
displaying white scars
on a leg that cannot bend.
Tales of a surgeon's scalpel.

Warming to his audience
he tells of how his youngest
is now an RAF flying instructor
therefore nearer to God by default.

He recognises ex-Sergeant Murphy,
a face from a past congregation.
Sits on his bed
and softly sings 'We'll meet again ...'

They gently sway. Old crooners
giving each other comradeship.
mock salutes and respect
to years scurrying behind their backs.

Monitors blip with detached efficiency.

The Auschwitz Tour Guide

Sun glassed and suited,
speaking in considered words.

She introduces us to pictures,
peopled with emaciated bodies
with almost transparent skin
stretched lampshade tight,
that look back with haunted eyes.

She shows us, a room size display case,
filled with human hair
that leaves us to imagine actualities
we have seen in movie newsreels
watching the silent buzz of barber's shears.

She shows us a picture
of children with forgotten names.
They bare their arms for camera
showing tattooed numbers
to the liberation photographer, and now, to us.

She guides us past
once electrified barbed wire,
demolished crematoria,
black headstones marking ash memories

And blossom laden fruit trees
with sad hanging branches
their leaves almost touching the ground.

Tourists take pictures
but they make sure they're never included.

Fish, Chips and Ice-Cream

In his council flat,
after he'd retired,
each Wednesday night I visited
doing what a dutiful son does.

Each visit we went through our routine
as if we'd learnt the script off by heart.

I'd buzz his Big-Ben door bell
that echoed the door's rattle
through the cold stone of the close.

He'd peek through his letter box
'Who's there?' he'd ask.

'It's me dad.' I'd reply to the clank of releasing bolts,
the rattle of safety chains
and the grind of the key in the lock.

Once inside he'd sit on *his* seat
and yet again tell me of the merits of *his* gas fire
as the palms of his hands skiffed together.

'Do you fancy a wee fish supper?' he'd ask.

'Yes, I'd reply, 'I'll go down to the chippy,
do you want a paper?' at this,
despite my protestations
he'd force a couple of pound into my hand.

And later on, when he heard the tinny chimes
of '*I love to go a wandering.*'

'Do you fancy an ice-cream?' he'd ask.

'Yes, I'd reply, 'I'll go down to the van,
Do you want any ginger?' at this,
again, he'd force a couple of pound into my hand.

One night he wandered from the script
telling me

'I know I don't show it, but I really do care.'
I hugged him like I was holding something fragile
frightened he might break.

He couldn't respond,
just a lingering look into my eyes.

As I made my way downstairs
I once again heard the clank and rattle and grind.

BRIAN WHITTINGHAM

The Mississippi Boys

On a Sunday this Mississippi boy
cruises in his Dodge pick up,
with powerboat trailing behind
along roads walled by still yellow wheat
to a Mississippi marina.

Scorching sun glints on chrome.

The drone or a red biplane.
A lazy speck in a clear blue sky.

Along the floating walkway
the supplies are carried onboard
cool-boxes, folding-chairs, sun-screen, towels etcetera

Hatches are battened down.

With his sandals, Bermuda shorts,
T-shirt, shades, baseball cap and fellow passengers
the captain for the day
gently introduces his power-boat
to the indifferent river.

The throttle easing the boat out with a gurgle
to join the other Mississippi boys
who, as if kids on vacation,
scoot up and down the river scudding foamy trails
left by fellow weekend mariners.

Occasionally they stop off
to meet their buddies in secluded bays

and anchor their boats on sandy shores.
The Mississippi boys
stand with the river lapping their knees
necking bottles of ice-cold beer
and smoking small black cigars

And like St Louis dudes
standing on any downtown street corner
the Mississippi boys chew the fat

and in the distance a long black barge
churns its way downstream.

The Still People

They could be called
street artistes,
these still-people who do nothing.
Their heads, faces and hands may be golden.
They may wear golden coats, top-hats, shoes,
have painted golden faces,
stand still frozen beside golden bicycles.

They will stare into nothingness
yet manage to see us
drop the odd coin into their baskets.

They may reciprocate
with the merest of ting-a-lings on their bicycle-bells.

The still-people do nothing.

Their heads, faces and hands may be grey.
They may wear grey cloaks, angel's wings, boots,
have painted grey faces,
stand still frozen on top of grey boxes.

They will stare into nothingness
yet manage to see us
drop the odd coin into their baskets.

They may reciprocate
with almost perceptible half bows.

We – an ever changing crowd
who think we are not easily impressed.
We – who are entertained by the still-people,

these street artistes
who will stand doing their nothing
that is for us, doing something.

The Never Ending Tea-Party

The 9 to 5 tourist guide
dressed in colonial patriot garb.
His silver buckled shoes
clump down the wooden walkway
onto the Boston-Tea-Party ship.

We follow –
Tourists from Chicago, Seattle, Texas, Oregon
and me, from Glasgow,
with a blue feather
sticking out of my hair,
given to cunningly disguise me as an Indian
like original tea-party participants.

The patriot shouts a potted history
asking questions
that the Americans eagerly respond to.

He yet again delivers the misdeeds of the British

'Taxation without representation,'

We, the crowd, holler in response
Dump the tea! – Into the sea!'

We chant this
as we throw kid-on sacks of tea into the sea,
with ropes tied to them
so they can be pulled up then thrown again
by the next participants
of this never ending Boston Tea Party.

And finally we are given a cup of tea to taste.

Final proof that these Americans
still haven't embraced
this most British of traditions.

Old Boys in Striped Pyjamas

He sits up
resting on his plumped up pillow.

'Can't even have a proper cigarette,' he says.

'A hernia operation is no big deal,'
I say, never having had one myself.

I know I'll be off my mark at 8:30 prompt.

'You can't even finish the meals ... too much.'

Another old boy with piles
shuffles over, smiles a sad smile.

'Used to work in the yards,' my dad shouts
thinking everyone is as deaf as him.

We all did at one time or another.

A septuagenarian
with a hearing aid like a suit-case
follows on, telling me
he was a painter but the fumes fucked his lungs.

And the old-boys in striped pyjamas
chew the fat.

Seattle Ducks

Our driver is dressed like a panto pirate,
with his plastic captain's hook on his arm
and black patch over one eye
he is all swash buckles and Oh-Arrs.

He calls us his, Duckineers,
as we board his amphibious vehicle.
He points to the open glassless windows
telling us they are emergency exits
that we can leap from, if in danger.

He tells us if we don't sing along to his songs
then we will have to walk de plank.

Some passengers have kazoo quackers
that puncture the air –

QUACK-QUACK, QUACK-QUACK.

He turns up the volume of 'We will rock you',
blaring from the Duck's loudspeakers
encouraging the passengers
to clap enthusiastically, sing along,
and wave cheerily at amused pedestrians
familiar with this local colour
as the duck's engine roars into life.

We pass the Space Needle,
Seattle's 60s icon poking
the blue sky with its dated, futuristic, architecture.

We pass the original Starbucks where the captain

instructs us to shout KERCHING! KERCHING!
Mimicking the sound of happy cash registers
that we must repeat every time we pass a Starbucks.
KERCHING! KERCHING! KERCHING!

QUACK-QUACK! QUACK-QUACK!

The Captain tells Emerald City tales ....

... of Mariner's home runs and
Pike Street flying fish and
Pioneer Square prospectors and
The final resting place for Cobain, Lee and Hendrix
And Bill Gates millions

and as a duckineer asks out loud

'HOW MANY HOMELESS ARE THERE IN SEATTLE?'

A sidewalk panhandler holds
a sign with the legend ...

BETCHA CAN'T HIT ME WITH A DOLLAR BILL

The Reminiscing Club

Archie shuffles
to his seat leaning heavy
on his aluminium walking stick.

Ina, with her Zimmer-frame
inches along with baby-steps
shakily dropping into her wheel-chair.

Old Ronald still manages
on his own with a gleam in his eye
and a green-stone ring on his finger.

At 78 rpm, a carer spins
the thick black plastic disc
on the repaired gramophone.

Its needle crackles
George Formby back to life.

He's *'Leaning on a Lamppost.'*

They listen, drumming fingers,
Tapping feet,
Smiling.

Archie remembers
teaching ballroom dancing
in the Orange-halls
where he used to sprinkle chalk-dust on the floor.

Ina remembers
being top soprano
in a 100 strong choir.
She tells of this in a whispery voice

and Old Ronald remembers
he learned banjo picking from Formby
at the pictures where he'd memorise
chords for his bedroom back home.

>   And as the carer spins Tommy Steele
>   and his *Little White Bull.*

Ronald remembers his old joke,
'*I stached my Moushave this morning,*'

… and they all laugh at the absurdity of it all.

The Man with the Wee Stick

Section by section
the murmur of instruments abate on cue.

The musicians rise to the lead violin
who bows almost imperceptibly
then they all sit – then they all rise ...

to the entrance of the man with the wee stick
who sports baggy black trousers,
a square shouldered velvet jacket,
pristine white shirted bow-tie
and black patent shoes.

He accidentally knocks over a music stand
that is saved from doing any damage
by an alert cellist.

The man with the wee stick
jokes with the audience –
'Should aim for a cheaper instrument the next time.'

The man with the wee stick
gently warms up the orchestra.

They respond,
with a slight shuffle of the feet
a slight rub of the music,
their protocol of applause.

The arrival of the young Italian Tenor,
stereotypical in demeanour and deportment,

who proceeds to give it laldy.
All eyes are fixed on the singer
and, the man with the wee stick
who hunches velvet shoulders,
crouches and focuses on the Tenor
with his very being
as if willing the notes to rise to a higher power.

After the finale
with much tapping of bows on music stands

some audience members toss flowers onto the stage
'Bravo – Bravo!'

Translated into Glaswegian,
'Gawn yirsel big man – Gawn yirsel!'

Coronary Care

On Christmas day
the nurses cover a makeshift table
with a paper towel tablecloth.

The white-gowned
patients from various words
introduce themselves to each other.

The nurses pour sparkling wine,
tune into a radio's Christmas cheer,
give everyone a paper hat.

      Frank, who's been told he's a 50/50 chance
      with his forthcoming bypass,
       smiles and jokes like there's no tomorrow.

      Anne, with her Christmas eve attack
      tells everyone, the last time she'd had red roses
      was when she'd had her first, 30 years before.

      James, who'd had a balloon inserted
      in an artery, slowly raises his leg in the air
      telling all, the doctors used helium by mistake.

The nurses, like magicians
lift the aluminium lids off the plates
revealing the steamed turkey dinners

And as glasses are raised for a toast –
outside the window
a seagull lands on the rim of a chimney pot
and momentarily peers into the ward.

Ghosts of the Titan Crane

The Titan Crane sits beside the empty dock,
with only its coat of blue paint
to shield it from the wind
that licks the flattened debris of the yard.

A small bus winds its way along the dockside
to the crane that's now a tourist attraction.

Inside, a spattering of passengers –
An ex-welder now living in California,
his brother, an ex-plater, now living in Dublin
and two other brothers, born and bred Bankies,
an ex-rigger and an ex-burner and their wives.

A lift silently ascends with the family
to a steel mesh platform 150 ft. in the air
that gives them a bird's-eye view of desolation.

In the jib's machine room
the gears and wires and wheels
of the once mighty crane
are still and silent and dead.

Apart from the whining wind,
the only sound comes from the flat-screen
that shows a celluloid shipyard
full of industry and noise and life.

The brothers and wives watch,
arms linked round each other's shoulders.

Outside they wander round the jib-deck
looking at the remnants of the end of the slipways
still poking their toes into the Clyde
where the great liners each made
an introductory bow towards Snodgrass field.

The wives see a barren panorama
of rubble and nothingness.

The brothers see ghosts of sprouting hulls
traversed by workers like boiler-suited ants,
and they hear a shrill horn piercing the air
and the clatter of thousands of steel-toe capped boots
worn by spectres stampeding towards the gates.

The Soapboy

The soapboy's honed scissors
snip snip snip to the rhythm
of the day's popular music
from the Salon's, always on, radio.

At the neck, he tucks in the gown
gently pumps the chair pedal
manoeuvres my head
to his required height and angle

He begins snip snip snipping –
snip snip snipping.

He chuckles, thinking aloud,
talking over my shoulder
to me, into the mirror in front.

'Coming straight from school
learning how to use a cut-throat,
lathering each customer's face,
they even had their own soap-mugs.'

The soapboy trims each hair
like a gardener keeping his shrubs
geometrically perfect
periodical snipping and combing –
snipping and combing.

'Of course heads are a lot cleaner now.'

He smiles making his point
by standing back with arms outstretched
and face grimacing
mimicking times past.

then effortlessly returns to his stance
snip snip snipping –
snip snip snipping

before finally doing the, hand held mirror
at the back of the head routine,
as he hands me a piece of torn off paper towel.

Mr Smarm and the Studio Audience

The studio audience
applaud like seals at the circus
being thrown morsels of fish.

We follow
the stage-manager's prompts
and electronic directives.

Like an army, formation-marching,
we applaud on command,
uniformly whistling, cheering and whooping.

Choreographed spontaneity.

MC Mr Smarm, with hair slicked back
and the sincerity of a used-car salesman
wrings his hands
like Uriah Heep dripping sugary words

and would have us believe
that mediocrity is talent
that necessitates our adulation

and we play our part
applauding thunderously because that's the thing to do,
and we know
because we are watching celebrities,
and because the overhead flashing sign tells us to do so.

The Last Ship Launch

Tugs manoeuvre for position
as if choreographed.
A band strikes up on the dockside.
Clusters of red and blue balloons drift with the breeze.

People cup hands over their eyes
looking towards the sun.
Amateur photographers take up position.

Stern first, the ship slowly slides
down the greased slipway, it breaks foamy waves
as it enters the water for the last time.

Small dust and rust clouds
rise above the shifting drag chains
followed by a daytime display of fireworks
whining and whizzing and exploding.

We can barely see them,
as if it may be disrespectful
to be seen to be too celebratory of the ending of an era.

Yet, it is the launching of a ship
on a river that was once lauded
for sending Clydebuilt to the four corners of the world.

What will today's river be known for
or will it be like its ships
remembered only for the glory of the past?

The Therapist

Is that Jake from Finnieston on the line?

Aye, that's right Erchie
an afore ah raise ma point
ah'd jist like tae say, yir show's pure spot on by the way.

Well thank you Jake, I'm glad you like it.

Listen Erchie, whit ah want tae talk aboot
is the guy who wis oan earlier
askin if he should play the piana
cause it soothed his nerves.

That's correct Jake
I'm a firm believer in someone
developing their musical talents,
especially if it assists relieving them
of the stress of living life in the fast lane, so to speak,
Introduces a piece of serenity, one might say
into the mundaneness of one's existence

Well, ah stey up above him
in the slow lane so tae speak
with not one smidgen of serenity one might say,
in the mundaneness of ma existence.

So what's the problem Jake?

The problemo big yin, is, that ah canny get tae sleep,
In fact the whole hoose canny get tae sleep.
In fact the whole fuckin sterrheid canny gat tae sleep,

Whit wi Liberace doonsterrs giein it mince oan the ivories

So ah's jist like tae say wan thing Erchie

thanks a bunch fur yir advice
thanks a fuckin bunch!

School Trip

Motorway lights loop shadows
on the three old men sitting,
composed on a silver-blue bus
as if in an old master's canvas.

The Normandy survivors
chat, suck pan drops and reflect
in the quiet company of sleepy head children.

They roll into a dozing Dover,
its spectral white cliffs
luminous in the waking dawn.

The ferry churns dark waters
heading towards Calais' blood red sun
beginning its daily cycle.
The school trip heads for ...

Normandy museums
with the tramp-tramp-tramp of Nazi jackboots,
the silk parachute wedding gown,
the graphitized remnants of Berlin's wall.

Normandy memorials
with vets and cadets reciting to Montgomery,
'They shall not grow old ...'
as they lay red-poppy wreaths.

Normandy cemeteries
with regular regimented marble crosses,
white as Belsen ashes,
and numerous as flakes of fallen snow.

Normandy beaches
with three old soldiers strolling
wearing their medals and black berets –
hands clasped behind their backs.

And on the beaches, kids crouch
and with their fingertips
write poems of reflection
in the warmth of the damp sand,
poems that will be collected by the evening tide
and washed into a past
that pains the old men to remember –
yet one they never wish to forget.

Vagabond Hotel

Opened windows overlook
the grassy courtyard crammed
with sun, trees and idyllic isolation.

Restless swallows
darting this way and that
with no time to stop
when one flies into a room
as if visiting
as if checking out the confines
before zipping back into open air.

Later on – a cat prowls,
prey clamped in its jaws,
broken wings, blood, limp feathers.

A low level jet intrudes,
buzzes overhead,
its whoosh lingers momentarily.

The Hotel Chevillon filled
with bits of themselves
artists have left behind
on paint peeling walls.

A plethora of artefacts
that somehow sit comfortably,
Angel Catchers and
A painting telling us, *This is the Truth* –
and so on and so on and so on …

All the while
into the wee small hours
artists in their studio,
husband and wife,
bring to life their Vagabond Highway
where the travellers, instead of cars, are people walking, running,
to and from a horizon that leads to who knows where?

The Hotel Chevillon is now an artist's foundation in Grez-sur-Loing in France. It was once an operational inn. Robert Louis Stevenson stayed there in 1877.

From Here to Eternity

In the art-house cinema –
the attendant with her flashlight switched off,
shows an old lady to a vacant seat in the front row.

The film has already started.

The old lady sits.
Puts her folded-up stick
on the ground beside her seat.

After the film's credits have run
when the houselights are switched on
the old lady feels for her stick.

The attendant guides her gently by the elbow
and escorts her to a side door.

Outside the cinema
the old lady peers into a mobile.
She deliberately dials
then asks me to check if she has done so correctly
reciting the digits from memory
as I check the phone's readout.

I tell her she has done good
and, curious, ask her what she thought of the film.

'I found it frightening,' she told me.
'I can't see films, I can only hear them
and when I heard the bombs exploding
it reminded me of the Clydebank Blitz'.

'15 people were killed in our street,' she told me.
Later that night, at home ...

I wondered what she remembered
when hearing Montgomery Clift's trumpet
piercing the hearts and the balmy air
of the packed bar
of Pearl Harbour's Bamboo Club

I wondered what she remembered
when hearing the waves crashing
over Lancaster and Kerr
and their illicit embrace on the wet sand,
wearing only their 50's swimsuits.

I wondered what she remembered.

The Catwalk Model

With her blond hair swept by the wind machine,
her ever so short red skirt
and Jimmy Choos complimenting
her shapely ankles

her designer bags,
with one precisely torn open
allow her Kellog's corn-flake box
and her Fairy washing up liquid bottle
to be strategically placed
as if having randomly fallen to the ground.

She seductively bends
whilst flirting her just so, made up eyes
with the camera's telephoto lens

that a glossy photographer manipulates
to ensure our new reality,
retouched appropriately,
can convince us that consumerism is all.

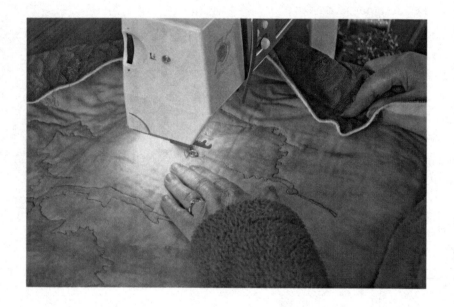

Sewing Fine Velvet

My mother spoke in her native tongue
whenever she became excited.
Words foreign to my young ears.

Worked with her embroidery ring
for endless hours.

Would say 'Tschuss' to departing friends.

I told her that when
I spoke her language at school
my friends called me a Nazi bastard
so I didn't want to learn anymore.

She cooked red cabbage and mashed potatoes
mixed with small cubes of ham
instead of pie, chips and beans.

She'd sit into the wee small hours
sewing fine velvet onto
plastic mesh hat frames
that a fat Jew with a fat cigar
and a smell of garlic from his breath,
would pay her money for.

She would sing soft foreign songs
When she dusted
and polished
and mended
and cooked

And sometimes mentioned
Oma and Opa or Friedel or Pieter
And a war of loss and shortages.

At Christmas my mother hummed Stille Nacht,
and placed small decorated bowls of nuts
at the base of the tree
and when I asked
why the cupboards were always stocked
with so many tins of food

she would tell me
that you never know what's round the corner.

Dining on Dreams

In a downtown Seattle nightclub
the staff are dressed with feathered boas, theatrical tiaras
and all the romance of 'turn of the century' France
in preparation for the in-house THEATRE ZINZANNI
that presents, in amongst the restaurant's table,
for the diner's pleasure,
a taste of a swirling, gastronomic whirlwind of comedy and
chaos

comprising of ...

The Master of Ceremonies –
Roberto Lopez

The M.C. called Mr. Zee or,
The Mighty Mexican Elvis ... El-Vez crooning
to the ladies in the audience while clutching
at his breaking heart throbbing
with well rehearsed passion
as Moulin Rouge style
waiters and waitresses glide
with the grace of ballet dancers
their silver serving trays
balanced perfectly
on the tips of extended fingers.

comprising of ...

The Clowns –
Los Excentricos

Zaza and Marceline, female clowns
faces fixed, painted smile and frown
With yellow and red billowy doll-like dresses,
their sprinkled silver dust
in the spot-lit air mingles ribbons of pale-blue smoke
and a man in the audience
blows bubbles like a child,
as Sylvestre, their male colleague
laughs his deranged laugh
he-he-heing through the silence
of their manic mimed routines.

comprising of ...
The Cabaret Singer –
Manuela Horn

The 7ft. tall Austrian Amazon
called Roxy for the purpose of tonight's show
wearing black leather laced stiletto boots
stockings, suspenders and split skirt
and tightly buttoned jacket revealing just enough cleavage,
her bunned hair under a jauntily tilted hat,
and Roxy sneers and toys with the men in the audience
taking one for a walk with a leash and collar round his neck
prior to unpinning and revealing with a flourish
her lusciously soft blond locks,
throwing her hat into the crowd
then piercing the air with a trademark yodel.

comprising of ...

The Dancer –
Joe Orrach

The pugilistic hoofer who,
somewhere between New York's 72nd and Columbus
and Seattle's 6th and Battery,
traded off his Welterweight Champion Title
for an elevated stage that rises slowly centre-floor
as he hurls aside his wig and jacket to reveal
a bald head and well honed frame wearing only
red-braces, black-trousers and shoes
that tap out a circular rhythm of
tapity-tap tapity-tap tapity-tap tapity-tap
becoming faster and faster and faster and faster
as dripping droplets of sweat shine silver
then explode in splashes under his hypnotic blurring feet.

comprising of ...

The evening's entertainment, all washed down with
1.5l Magnums of Dom Perignon
@ $120 a bottle.

And the audience stand and stomp and whistle and clap and
holler and embrace
having dined on dreams
before the houselights of reality are once again switched on.

Histogram Man

I ask if I should upgrade.

Histogram man smiles,
'It doesn't matter,' he says,
'It's only a box that captures light,
cameras all do the same thing.
Learn to observe light, that's the ticket.'

He tells me, 'Clouds are good.
They give form – paint the landscape with light.'

He tells me, 'Rain is good,' 'Look,' he says,
pointing to the foreboding sky
above the road, ribboned through the glen,
'It's as if the rainclouds are following us,' he laughs,
'Maybe they'll hug the 3 Sisters for a while – leave *us* alone.'

He points to a spot beside the river,
'This is a good place,' he says,
eyeing the familiar of The Weeping Glen.

My tripod's feet rest in the mud,
that soaks through my shoes.

I adjust the camera's settings as instructed,
film speed, aperture, shutter speed.
I fix on my Grad filter.

My pupil's eyes try to gauge the correct point of focus,
and watch the shifting shapes of clouds and light
coat the top of Buachaille Etive Mor.
Click!

He shows me how to check the histogram.
Explains it's a graph of shade and light.

It's as if it empowers me, godlike,
to manipulate the finished image to my own liking.

And while I'm absorbed in the process
transient snappers, who also know the good spots,
momentarily hunker down, click click click,
then disappear to their next location.

The histogram man gives them knowing smiles,
waits patiently to interrupt my enthusiasm,
before moving on.

'Do you not get fed up coming to the same places all the time?'
    I ask.

'They're never the same,' he says, 'The light makes sure of that.'

The Breakdown

The draughtsman sat at the CNC programming machine.

Unsure of his trigonometry
he puzzled over whether to choose
Polar or Cartesian co-ordinates.

As he stroked his chin in thought
the printer assumed a life of its own,
made a buzzing sound
and spilled out paper over his lap
as if he were centre stage in a Laurel and Hardy scene.

The other draughtsmen sniggered.

They thought it was about time
their colleague was brought down a peg or two
because he continually reminded them
that he'd been a Big-Noise in his last place of work.

As the paper continued to pile up,
a foreman burst into the office
telling the draughtsman
he'd better come down to the shop-floor, toot-sweet,
as his job had, had an almighty fuck-up
that needed to be fixed PDQ.

The draughtsman's phone rang.
He lifted it from its cradle
and as he listened his hand began to shake
and tears slowly wet his cheeks.

An older colleague
put a coat over his shoulders,
took him outside the office ,
took him away from the factory

down to the local park where they sat on a bench.

A passer-by stopped
asked if they wanted to feed the ducks
and without waiting for an answer
left them some slices of bread.

The draughtsman tore off small pieces
and threw them, watching them plop into the pond.

His older colleague lit up his pipe
and remarked that the clouds looked as if they were clearing up.

Titian's Head in a Welder's Helmet

In Kelvingrove's Gallery: Titian's head,
in a 16th. Century painting.
An adulteress pleading before Christ
as a mob make ready with stones of justice.

The head's impassive eyes
on the edge of the rabble,
looks – not at the woman – but at you;
challenging you to be a sinner
or the first to throw a stone perhaps?

A painting for Venetian Nobles.

In Glasgow's Transport Museum: Titian's head,
replicated by a 20th century Port Glasgow artisan,
this time in a shipyard mural.

Titian's head in a welder's helmet –
lights his cigarette
from the glowing end of a hot electrode.

Around him men smoke pipes and cigarettes,
heat tea-cans with burning-torches,
scuttle round heavy flanged ducting
like Stanley Spencer artisans

while Titian's head
again, holds his stare
looking at you, this time
challenging you to be friend or foe
or to go about your business as a fellow worker perhaps?

A painting for the proletariat.

Coming Home to Her Own

Is what Cunard's CEO said
as we sipped complimentary champagne.
My son and I in our smartest suits.
We stood in the 60's style ballroom
that would never know
our shiny black shoes dance the years away.

The QE2's final Greenock visit
before retiring to her Dubai rest-home.
Us ex-workers on board
destined for a less salubrious old age.

And out on deck
we watched the flotilla of little ships
shoot water cannons in salute,
hoot their horns and wave their flags
in recognition of our importance

the Red Arrows scrawled the sky
with coloured tracer trails
that zoomed and whooshed above our heads.

In the Mauretania restaurant,
'God save the Queen!' A murmured repetition
with clinking glasses greeting the Captain's toast.

Prior to   *Grilled Salmon Steak & Seared Scallops*
                   Crushed Tomato Chutney
                   Artichoke & Tarragon Reduction
                   Forked Red Skin Potato
washed down with   *Santa Carolina Cabernet Sauvignon*

with the white-gloved waiter
discreetly brushing off the few stray crumbs
that dared blemish the embroidered finery
of the pristine tablecloth

and for some reason I remember
cans of scalding tea and cheese pieces.
The work's shrill whistle at the tea-break's end
and the freezing fabrication shed
and the filth
and the mayhem
of the Black Squad.

The Fish Market Philosopher

The fish market philosopher
holds court with his audience
to a backdrop of iced, cold, wet, fish

He wears orange waders,
sports a red octopus tattoo,
its tentacles snaking round his arm
and a Seattle smile
as large as the Pacific Northwest.

And instead of selling iced, cold, wet, fish
he sells ...

Live Manila Clams
fresh Alaskan Silver Salmon fillets
jumbo Caribbean Rock Lobster Tails
blue Marlin steaks and Yellow Finned tuna

and when a customer swallows his sale's pitch,
hook line and sinker,
and picks a preferred fish,
the fish-market philosopher
hurls the King Salmon through the air
into the hands of a colleague behind the counter
who, like a soccer goalie,
secures his catch in a sheet of greaseproof paper.

On cue, another fishmonger
hurls a stuffed cloth fish back into the crowd
who duck and dive for cover.

Children squeal, parents laugh, cameras click.

All the while
another colleague continually tops up the display
with spades of fresh flaked-ice.

When a sale is made
One fishmonger hollers 'Sockeye – Oregon!'
A colleagues echoes
'Sockeye – Oregon!'

Another hollers 'Seaweed cocktails – hold the seaweed!'
sweeping his hand toward potted crab delicacy,

then they all begin a hollering as if
fish in a feeding frenzy.

'WaaaaaaaaaaaaaaaaaaaaaaaaaayHA!'

And when I ask him why he
looks so happy when working
he tells me how you feel inside
is shaped by the language you use
because it becomes your experience
so they always holler positives
even when they're feeling negative.

'WaaaaaaaaaaaaaaaaaaaaaaaaaayHA!'

It's all up to you, no one else.
We are all responsible for what we experience in life!
He tell me assuredly
as a Red-King crab flies over our heads.

'Red Crab – Montana!'

'WaaaaaaaaaaaaaaaaaaaaaaaaaayHA!'

Some other books published by **LUATH** PRESS

Bunnets n Bowlers: A Clydeside Odyssey

Brian Whittingham
ISBN 978-1906307-94-3 PBK £8.99

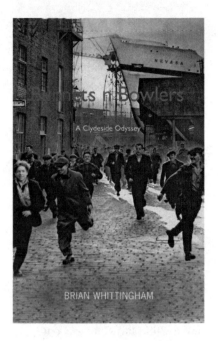

'Ach, bit thers nae need tae worry,
ah'll get yi a joab in the yards,
yi'll be fixed up fur life
so yi wull, fixed up fir life'

Every ship has a story, and so does every shipbuilder, whether they are bowler hats, the foremen whose job it was to make sure deadlines were met, or bunnets, the skilled artisans that did the graft.

Meet the characters of The Black Squad: Sam Abbott, the knicker knocker from Duntocher; Wild Bill Hickok, the card shark; Irish Pat, the burner who likes his bevvy too much, and many more. They've spent their lives together in John Brown's shipyard sharing in the hilarity and tragedy of their work.

Brian Whittingham started his career in the Clydeside shipyards at just 15 years old when a job in the yards was for life. *Bunnets n Bowlers* follows this Clydeside odyssey, familiar to so many, from smart-arsed apprentice to skilled artisan and celebrates the humour and camaraderie of an ailing profession.

A vivid account of the rich and varied life in the yards.
THE EVENING TIMES

This paperback celebrates the Clyde shipyards in their heyday – not achieved through rose-tinted glasses but via the often gritty recollections of those who spent a large part of their lives in these very shipyards.
SCOTS MAGAZINE

The poetry achieves an immediacy that is difficult to achieve in weighty tombs of labour history.
HISTORY SCOTLAND

Drink the Green Fairy

Brian Whittingham

ISBN 978-1-842820-45-2 PBK £8.99

The last time I drank the Green Fairy was twenty-eight years ago on my stag night. I ended up upside-down, having been deposited in a rubbish bin with my legs sticking up in the air in Glasgow's Queen Street station.

BRIAN WHITTINGHAM

Brian Whittingham walks the streets of Glasgow, dips into people's lives and delves into the world of the Impressionist painters. The poems are quick snapshots, focusing on the particular of the ordinary and yet widening the gaze to the universal in life. Colour is not just splashed across the canvases of the painter's lives he explores, but finds its way into the lives of all those he encounters. With his own bold brush strokes Whittingham mixes the territories of high art and city streets, making both equally significant in the make-up of daily lives.

Here is a collection which packages Glasgow (and Paris flung in for good measure) using microcosmic insights and incidences to create, through an integrity of humanity, the universality most writers would sell their soul for... the finest collection of poetry I've read in years.

DES DILLON

His poetry is not 'nice'... but it has a balance and poise to simultaneously delight in life, and weep over it.

CHRIS DOLAN

A warm and attractive collection, with a characteristic plend of sympathetic observation and sharp social comment.

EDWIN MORGAN

Never Mind the Captions

Alistair Findlay

ISBN 978-1-906817-89-3 PBK £7.99

*We come here every year with Viking
    Tours
– The Axe Factory Managers'
    Convention –
all square-dancing and eyes-bulging
    contests.
Look! That's me, the current world
    champion.*

ALISTAIR FINDLAY on the mysterious
850-year-old Lewis Chessmen

Join Alistair Findlay on an off-beat
tour of Scotland, from museum
artifacts to public pieces of art,
where he captures the humorous,
passionate, and sometimes biting
voices of some of our national
treasures.

*Alistair Findlay has not only
articulated the silent unspoken
questions which people ask of
museum pieces and cultural icons,
he lets the objects answer back,
to the delight and entertainment
of the reader.*

DR ELSPETH KING,
Director, Stirling Smith Art Gallery
and Museum

*This off-beat guide to Scotland's
history and heritage captures the
humorous, passionate, and sometimes
mordant voices of the country's public
treasures.*

THE HERALD

*Findlay is one of Scotland's sharpest
poets...* [Never Mind the Captions]
*is a big book and a wonderfully
subversive, sideways look at some of
the public emblems of Scottish history.*
THE MORNING STAR

100 Favourite Scottish Poems

Edited by Stewart Conn
ISBN 978 1905222 61 2 PBK £7.99

Poems to make you laugh. Poems to make you cry. Poems to make you think. Poems to savour. Poems to read out loud. To read again, and again. Scottish poems. Old favourites. New favourites. 100 of the best.

Scotland has a long history of producing outstanding poetry. From the humblest but-and-ben to the grandest castle, the nation has a great tradition of celebration and commemoration through poetry. *100 Favourite Scottish Poems* – incorporating the top 20 best-loved poems as selected by a BBC Radio Scotland listener poll – ranges from ballads to Burns and from 'Cuddle Doon' to 'The Jeelie Piece Song'.

Edited by Stewart Conn, poet and inaugural recipient of the Institute of Contemporary Scotland's Iain Crichton Smith Award for services to literature (2006). Published in association with the Scottish Poetry Library.

100 Favourite Scottish Love Poems

Edited by Stewart Conn
ISBN 978-1-906307-66-0 PBK £7.99

Poems of passion. Poems of compassion. Poems of cherishing. Poems of yearning. Poems that celebrate and illuminate. Poems vibrant with the tenderness and heartbreak of love.

Embracing love reciprocated and love unrequited , this selection ranges from irrepressible optimism to longing and loss; from lovers' abandon to parental affection. There are poems for every lover and loved one to savour and share, and to touch the heart. But leaving plenty room for humour and a whiff of sour grapes.

Stewart Conn mines Scotland's rich seam of love poetry in its different tongues - from traditional ballads, Burns and Scott to MacCaig, MacLean, Morgan and the vitality of Liz Lochhead and Jackie Kay; from 'Barbara Allan', 'The Blythesome Bridal' and 'Lassie Lie Near Me' to 'Hot Chick', 'Yeah Yeah Yeah' and 'Out with my Loves on a Windy Day'.

More poetry from Luath press

Scunnered: Slices of Scottish Life in Seventeen Gallus Syllables
Des Dillon
ISBN 978-1-908373-01-4 PBK £7.99

A Map for the Blind
Rab Wilson
ISBN 978-1-906817-82-4 PBK £8.99

Thi 20:09
Mark Thompson
ISBN 978-1-906817-82-4 PBK £6.99

100 Favourite Scottish Football Poems
Edited by Alistair Findlay
ISBN 978-1-906307-03-5 PBK £7.99

100 Favourite Scottish Poems to Read Aloud
Edited by Gordon Jarvie
ISBN 978-1-906307-011 PBK £7.99

Accent o the Mind
Rab Wilson
ISBN 978-1-905222-32-2 PBK £8.99

Bad Ass Raindrop
Kokumo Rocks
ISBN 978-1-842820-14-1 PBK £6.99

Bard fae the Building Site
Mark Thompson
ISBN 978-1-906307-14-1 PBK £7.99

Bodywork
Dilys Rose
ISBN 978-1-905222-93-3 PBK £8.99

Brainheart
Paraig MacNeil
ISBN 978-1-905222-31-5 PBK £6.99

Burning Whins
Liz Niven
ISBN 978-1-842820-74-2 PBK £8.99

Chuckies fir the Cairn
Edited by Rab Wilson
ISBN 978-1-906817-05-3 PBK £8.99

Dancing with Big Eunice
Alistair Findlay
ISBN 978-1-906817-28-8 PBK £7.99

From the Ganga to the Tay
Bashabi Fraser
ISBN 978-1-906307-95-0 PBK £8.99

Luath Kilmarnock Edition: Poems Chiefly in the Scottish Dialect
Robert Burns
ISBN 978-1-906307-67-7 HBK £15

Luath Burns Companion
John Cairney
ISBN 978-1-906817-85-5 PBK £9.99

North End of Eden
Christine De Luca
ISBN 978-1-906817-35-9 PBK £8.99

Not Just Moonshine
Tessa Ransford
ISBN 978-1-906307-77-6 PBK £12.99

Picking Brambles
Des Dillon
ISBN 978-1-842820-21-6 PBK £6.99

The Shard Box
Liz Niven
ISBN 978-1-906817-62-6 PBK £7.99

Details of these and other books published by Luath Press can be found at:
www.luath.co.uk

Luath Press Limited

committed to publishing well written books worth reading

LUATH PRESS takes its name from Robert Burns, whose little collie Luath (*Gael.*, swift or nimble) tripped up Jean Armour at a wedding and gave him the chance to speak to the woman who was to be his wife and the abiding love of his life. Burns called one of 'The Twa Dogs' Luath after Cuchullin's hunting dog in Ossian's *Fingal*. Luath Press was established in 1981 in the heart of Burns country, and is now based a few steps up the road from Burns' first lodgings on Edinburgh's Royal Mile.

Luath offers you distinctive writing with a hint of unexpected pleasures.

Most bookshops in the UK, the US, Canada, Australia, New Zealand and parts of Europe either carry our books in stock or can order them for you. To order direct from us, please send a £sterling cheque, postal order, international money order or your credit card details (number, address of cardholder and expiry date) to us at the address below. Please add post and packing as follows: UK – £1.00 per delivery address; overseas surface mail – £2.50 per delivery address; overseas air-mail – £3.50 for the first book to each delivery address, plus £1.00 for each additional book by airmail to the same address. If your order is a gift, we will happily enclose your card or message at no extra charge.

Luath Press Limited
543/2 Castlehill
The Royal Mile
Edinburgh EH1 2ND
Scotland
Telephone: 0131 225 4326 (24 hours)
Fax: 0131 225 4324
email: sales@luath.co.uk
Website: www.luath.co.uk